BRILLIANCE IN PURPOSE

Brilliance in Purpose

DAVID OLUBIYI

Dabim Support Services Inc.

Contents

Copyright — vi
Dedication — vii
Introduction: — ix
Overview of Alex's Story — xi
Purpose of the Book — xiii
How to Use This Book: — xv

One — Childhood and Family Life — 1

Two — Medical Education and Residency — 8

Three — The Importance of Support: Alex's Journey with his Partner — 13

Four — Facing Setbacks — 18

Five — Achievements and Contributions — 21

Six — Life Beyond Medicine — 24

Conclusion — 27
Lessons Learned — 29
Final Thoughts — 31
Acknowledgement — 33

Dedication

This book is dedicated to the memory of my beloved parents; Amos and Taiwo Osunbiyi, who have passed away but continue to live on in my heart and mind. They were my constant source of love, guidance, and inspiration, and their unwavering support allowed me to pursue my dreams and aspirations. I am forever grateful for the memories we shared and the lessons they taught me. May their legacy continue to shine bright and may they rest in eternal peace.

Introduction:

Alex was always an exceptional individual. Growing up, he had a curious mind and a thirst for knowledge that led him to excel in his studies and pursue a career in medicine. Despite facing numerous obstacles and setbacks along the way, Alex remained determined to achieve his goals and make a difference in the world.

This book tells the story of Alex's remarkable journey from his childhood to his current position as a world-renowned expert in his field. It explores the challenges he faced, the triumphs he achieved, and the lessons he learned along the way.

In the following chapters, we will delve into Alex's family background, education, and medical training, as well as the support he received from his wife, Sarah. We will also examine the setbacks and failures he encountered, and how he overcame them with resilience and determination.

Throughout his career, Alex has made significant contributions to the medical field, including groundbreaking research and innovative surgical procedures. We will explore these achievements in detail, as well as his personal interests, family life, and philanthropic endeavors.

Through Alex's story, we can learn valuable lessons about perseverance, resilience, and the power of support. It is our hope that this book will inspire readers to pursue their own passions and strive for excellence in all aspects of their lives.

Overview of Alex's Story

Alex's story is one of perseverance, determination, and triumph. Despite facing numerous obstacles throughout his life, he was able to achieve great success in both his personal and professional endeavors.

Alex grew up in a working-class family, where his parents instilled in him the importance of hard work and education. Despite facing financial hardships and societal challenges, Alex excelled in his studies and went on to pursue a career in medicine.

During his medical education and residency, Alex faced numerous challenges, including difficult surgeries, long hours, and intense criticism from his peers. However, he persevered and eventually became a world-renowned expert in his field, thanks to his dedication and hard work.

Outside of work, Alex also achieved great success, including winning prestigious awards, writing a bestselling book, and serving as a mentor and advocate for underserved communities.

Throughout his journey, Alex was supported by his loving wife, who stood by his side through both his triumphs and setbacks.

Alex's story is a testament to the power of resilience, determination, and hard work. It serves as an inspiration to anyone facing challenges in their own lives, and shows that with perseverance and dedication, anything is possible.

Purpose of the Book

The purpose of this book is to share Alex's story of perseverance, determination, and triumph, and to inspire others to overcome their own challenges and achieve their goals. By sharing Alex's journey, the book aims to motivate and encourage readers to pursue their passions and dreams, despite any obstacles they may face.

Additionally, the book seeks to provide insight and inspiration for those pursuing a career in medicine or other challenging fields, by highlighting the hard work, dedication, and sacrifices required to achieve success in these areas.

Overall, the purpose of this book is to inspire and empower readers to embrace their own journey, and to provide a roadmap for achieving success in the face of adversity.

How to Use This Book:

This book is designed to be a comprehensive and engaging account of Alex's remarkable journey. Whether you are a medical professional, a student, or simply someone interested in the story of a remarkable individual, this book offers valuable insights and inspiration.

Each chapter focuses on a different aspect of Alex's life, and can be read independently or as part of a larger narrative. The book is divided into three main sections: Alex's background and education, his career as a doctor and researcher, and his achievements outside of work.

The book can be used in a variety of ways, including:

1. As a source of inspiration: Alex's story is one of resilience, determination, and perseverance. Readers can draw inspiration from his experiences and apply his lessons to their own lives.

2. As a study tool: Medical students and professionals can gain insights into the challenges and triumphs of a successful medical career, as well as the latest research and surgical techniques.

3. As a personal account: Alex's story is a deeply personal one, and readers can gain a deeper understanding of his motivations, passions, and struggles.

Throughout the book, we encourage readers to reflect on their own lives and experiences, and consider how they can apply Alex's lessons to their own journey. We hope this book will inspire readers to pursue their passions, overcome obstacles, and strive for excellence in all aspects of their lives.

Chapter One

Childhood and
Family Life

Once upon a time, there was a brilliant young boy named Alex. Alex was a child prodigy who showed exceptional intelligence and talent from a very young age. His parents noticed his extraordinary abilities and encouraged him to pursue his interests.

Alex grew up in a close-knit family, with both parents and an older sister. His parents were both immigrants who came to the United States to pursue better opportunities. They instilled in him a strong work ethic, and encouraged him to pursue his interests and passions. Alex's father worked as a factory worker, while his mother was a homemaker who also took care of the family's small business. Despite their limited resources, they made sure that Alex had access to opportunities that would allow him to develop his talents. This included music lessons, art classes, and exposure to books and other educational resources. The support and guidance of his family played a crucial role in shaping Alex's early years and helping him develop his exceptional abilities.

As immigrants to the United States, Alex's parents faced numerous challenges and obstacles. They had to navigate a new culture, language, and way of life, while also providing for their family. Despite these difficulties, they persevered and worked hard to build a better life for themselves and their children.

Growing up, Alex witnessed his parents' resilience and determination firsthand. He saw how they overcame adversity through hard work and perseverance, and how they approached challenges as opportunities for growth. Their example likely played a significant role in shaping his own mindset and approach to adversity.

Through their own experiences with hardship and resilience, Alex's parents taught him the value of persistence and the importance of bouncing back from setbacks. This lesson was integral to Alex's ability to deal with failure and keep striving for excellence in his career and personal life.

Alex was always curious about everything around him. He loved reading books, solving puzzles, and experimenting with new things. He excelled in all his classes and was always at the top of his class. He was not only intelligent but also had a great sense of humour, which made him popular among his classmates.

As Alex grew older, his talents became even more apparent. He was an exceptional musician, an outstanding athlete, and a gifted artist. His teachers and parents were amazed at his ability to excel in so many different areas.

His ability to remain grounded despite his success is a testament to his strong character and values. He understood that success is not just about achieving great things but also about maintaining a positive attitude and outlook on life.

His humility and dedication to self-improvement were evident in his actions. He never took his accomplishments for granted and was always looking for ways to push himself further. He sought out feedback and constructive criticism to help him grow, and he was not afraid to admit when he made mistakes.

His eagerness to learn new things and take on challenges also made him a valuable team member and leader. He was not content with staying in his comfort zone but instead sought out new experiences and perspectives that could benefit himself and his team. This attitude helped him to develop a broad range of skills and knowledge that he could draw upon in different situations..

As he approached high school, Alex began to think about his future. He knew he wanted to continue his education and pursue a career that would allow him to use his talents to help others. After much consideration, he decided to become a doctor.

Alex's relentless pursuit of his dream was characterized by his unwavering commitment and dedication. He poured endless hours into his studies, leaving no stone unturned in his quest for knowledge and excellence. He was determined to achieve success, and his work ethic was a testament to his unwavering resolve.

In addition to his academic pursuits, Alex recognized the importance of gaining practical experience in his field. He sought out volunteer opportunities at hospitals and clinics, where he could learn from experienced professionals and gain hands-on knowledge of the medical field. Alex was not content with simply mastering theoretical concepts; he wanted to understand the practical realities of healthcare and how to provide the best possible care to patients.

Furthermore, Alex's passion for helping others extended beyond his academic and professional goals. He felt a deep sense of responsibility to use his skills and knowledge to make a positive impact on society. To this end, he founded his own charity to provide medical care to those in need. This initiative demonstrated his compassion and selflessness, and his commitment to helping those who were less fortunate.

Alex's tireless work ethic, dedication, and altruism were the hallmarks of his character. His achievements were not just a result of his intelligence and talent, but also his willingness to put in the hard work and effort required to reach his goals. His passion for medicine and his desire to make a difference in people's lives inspired those around him, and his legacy of hard work and compassion continues to inspire others to this day.

After completing his undergraduate studies in biology, Alex was accepted into a highly competitive medical program. He excelled in his coursework, and was known for his exceptional knowledge and clinical skills. During his residency, Alex worked tirelessly to gain hands-on experience in a variety of medical specialties. He was particularly interested in his area of specialization, and spent long hours studying and researching to deepen his knowledge and hone his skills.

Despite the demanding nature of his medical training, Alex remained dedicated to his patients and their families. He was known for his compassion and bedside manner, and went above and beyond to ensure that his patients received the best possible care. This commitment to patient care became a hallmark of his career, and helped to set him apart as a leader in the field.

Throughout his medical education and residency, Alex faced numerous challenges and obstacles. He had to balance the demands of his coursework and clinical work with his personal life and relationships. He also had to contend with the emotional toll of working with seriously ill patients and their families.

However, through it all, Alex remained focused on his goals and committed to his chosen path. He recognized that his medical education and residency were essential steps on the path to achieving his dreams, and he worked tirelessly to make the most of these opportunities. His dedication and hard work during this time laid the foundation for his later success as a world-renowned expert in his field.

Alex's journey began after his graduation from medical school. His passion and dedication to his profession were evident right from the beginning, and his abilities quickly became apparent. Alex's exceptional surgical skills and compassionate approach to patient care made him stand out from his peers.

As a leading expert in his field, Alex faced a great deal of pressure to perform at the highest level. He was constantly pushing himself to learn more, refine his skills, and deliver the best possible outcomes for his patients. However, this level of intensity sometimes left him open to criticism and scrutiny from others in the medical community.

One criticism that Alex sometimes faced was that he was too focused on his research and academic pursuits, at the expense of his clinical work. Some of his colleagues felt that he was too focused on advancing his own career and reputation, and not focused enough on the day-to-day demands of patient care.

Another challenge that Alex faced was in managing the expectations of his patients and their families. As a leading expert in his field, patients and families often came to him with high expectations and complex medical issues. While Alex always did his best to deliver the best possible care and outcomes, sometimes these expectations were difficult to manage.

Despite these challenges and criticisms, Alex remained committed to his patients and his work as a doctor. He recognized that the medical field was complex and constantly evolving, and that there were always opportunities for growth and learning. He also recognized that criticism was a natural part of the field, and used it as an opportunity to reflect on his own work and make improvements where necessary.

Overall, Alex's dedication to his patients, his commitment to excellence, and his willingness to learn and grow in the face of criticism helped to set him apart as a leader in the medical community.

His colleagues and patients alike soon took notice of his abilities, and Alex began to earn their respect and admiration. It was clear that he had a unique gift for surgery, and his dedication to improving his craft only solidified this reputation.

Early in his career, Alex developed an innovative surgical technique for the treatment of a rare and complex condition. The condition, which affected the heart and lungs, was previously thought to be untreatable. However, through his research and experimentation, Alex developed a new approach that allowed him to successfully operate on the affected area and restore normal function.

This ground-breaking surgery quickly gained worldwide attention, and Alex was invited to present his findings at medical conferences and symposia around the globe. He became known as a leading expert in the treatment of this rare condition, and his surgical technique was adopted by other doctors and medical centers around the world.

Over time, Alex continued to refine and improve his surgical technique, incorporating the latest research and technology to deliver even better outcomes for his patients. He also became known for his innovative approaches to other types of surgeries, and was often sought out for his expertise in difficult and complex cases.

Through his ground-breaking surgical work, Alex helped to change the face of modern medicine, and his legacy continues to inspire and inform medical practice to this day.

Over time, Alex became known as a world-renowned expert in his field. His surgical techniques and approach were unparalleled, and he had the ability to transform the lives of his patients in ways that few other surgeons could match.

Throughout his career, Alex remained humble and focused on his patients, always striving to provide the best care possible. His tireless dedication to his craft and unwavering commitment to patient care were an inspiration to all those who knew him, and he continued to make a lasting impact in the world of medicine..

Throughout his career, Alex helped save countless lives, using his expertise and skill to perform complex surgeries and procedures that transformed his patients' lives. He approached each case with empathy, compassion, and a deep understanding of the human body and the challenges faced by those who were ill or injured. His unwavering commitment to his patients and his profession was evident in every aspect of his work, from his meticulous attention to detail in the operating room to his advocacy for healthcare reform and access to quality care.

Alex's impact on the medical field was profound and far-reaching. He was a mentor to countless aspiring doctors and surgeons, sharing his knowledge and expertise to help them achieve their own goals and dreams. His legacy of excellence and dedication continues to inspire new generations of medical professionals, reminding us all of the profound impact that one person can have on the world through hard work, dedication, and a commitment to helping others..

Despite all his success, Alex never forgot where he came from. He remained humble and always remembered the people who helped him along the way. He continued to give back to his community and mentor young people who showed promise in medicine.

Chapter Two

Medical Education and Residency

As Alex continued on his journey, he faced many challenges and obstacles. There were times when he felt overwhelmed and unsure of himself, but he always found the strength to persevere.

As Alex's career began to take off, he found himself increasingly pulled in different directions, trying to balance his demanding work schedule with his personal life. It was a challenge that many successful professionals faced, and Alex was no exception. He found himself working long hours, often late into the night, and struggling to make time for the people and activities that he loved.

Despite the many demands on his time, Alex recognized the importance of maintaining a strong support network of family and friends. He knew that these connections were crucial to his overall well-being and mental health, and he made a conscious effort to prioritize them. He set aside time each week to catch up with loved ones, whether it was a phone call, a dinner date, or a weekend outing. He also made sure to take breaks from work, to pursue hobbies and activities that he enjoyed, and to recharge his batteries.

While Alex was certainly a dedicated and accomplished doctor, he also had a number of achievements outside of his medical career. One of his greatest passions was running, and he was an accomplished long-distance runner in his free time. He often participated in marathons and other races, and was known for his impressive endurance and dedication to training.

In addition to his athletic pursuits, Alex was also a prolific writer and researcher. He authored several influential papers and articles in medical journals, and was invited to speak at conferences and symposia around the world. He also served as a mentor and advisor to a number of young doctors and medical students, helping to guide and inspire the next generation of medical professionals.

Outside of medicine, Alex was also deeply committed to his family and community. He was a devoted husband and father, and spent much of his free time volunteering with local organizations and charities. He was particularly passionate about advocating for increased access to healthcare for underserved populations, and was a frequent guest speaker at community events and rallies.

Alex was also an avid traveler and adventurer. He had a deep love of exploring new places and cultures, and often embarked on international trips with his family and friends. Some of his favourite destinations included remote wilderness areas and exotic locales, where he could immerse himself in local traditions and customs.

In addition to his travels, Alex was also a talented artist and musician. He played several instruments, including the guitar and piano, and often composed his own music. He also had a talent for drawing and painting, and his artwork was featured in several local galleries and exhibitions.

Throughout his life, Alex remained deeply committed to personal growth and self-improvement. He was an avid reader and learner, constantly seeking out new information and insights to help him become a better doctor, athlete, artist, and person. He also valued his relationships with family and friends, and made a point of staying connected with loved ones despite his busy schedule.

Overall, Alex's achievements outside of work were a reflection of his multi-faceted personality and his passion for life. Whether he was running marathons, exploring new cultures, creating art and music, or simply spending time with loved ones, he was always fully engaged and committed to making the most of every moment.

However, balancing his professional and personal life was not always easy, and Alex faced many challenges along the way. But he never lost sight of what was truly important: the people and relationships that mattered most to him. He knew that success was not just about achieving career goals or accumulating accolades, but also about building a fulfilling and meaningful life outside of work.

Through his example, Alex demonstrated the importance of maintaining a healthy work-life balance and the benefits that came from prioritizing personal relationships. He showed that success was not just about what you achieved, but also about how you lived your life, and the impact you had on those around you. His commitment to both his professional and personal pursuits made him a role model for others, inspiring them to pursue their own dreams while still prioritizing the things that truly mattered.

Another challenge Alex faced was dealing with failure. Dealing with failure can be a difficult experience for anyone, even someone as talented and accomplished as Alex. But he didn't let setbacks and disappointments get the best of him. Instead, he learned to approach these experiences with a growth mindset. He recognized that failure was a natural part of the learning process, and that it provided valuable opportunities for personal and professional growth.

Despite his many achievements, Alex also faced a number of setbacks and challenges along the way. One of the biggest obstacles he encountered was during his residency, when he was diagnosed with a serious medical condition that required him to take a leave of absence from his training. This was a difficult setback for Alex, who had always prided himself on his physical and mental resilience.

During his recovery, Alex faced a number of setbacks and complications, including a prolonged hospital stay and a lengthy rehabilitation period. However, he remained determined to return to his medical training as soon as possible, and worked tirelessly to regain his strength and stamina.

Another setback that Alex faced was a difficult case he encountered early in his career as a surgeon. Despite his best efforts, the patient ultimately did not survive, and Alex was left feeling deeply discouraged and frustrated. However, he learned from this experience and used it as motivation to become an even better doctor, striving to improve his skills and knowledge every day.

Overall, these setbacks were difficult and challenging for Alex, but he used them as opportunities for growth and learning. Through hard work and perseverance, he was able to overcome these obstacles and emerge even stronger and more determined to succeed.

Alex believed that failure wasn't the end of the road, but rather a chance to learn and improve. He used each setback as a stepping stone to the next level of his career, learning from his mistakes and using the lessons he learned to refine his approach and achieve even greater success. This mindset allowed him to stay motivated and focused, even when faced with difficult challenges.

Alex's ability to view failure as a catalyst for growth is a valuable lesson for anyone striving to achieve success. It's a reminder that setbacks and disappointments are an inevitable part of life, but how we choose to respond to them is what sets us apart. By embracing failure as an opportunity for growth and using it as motivation to keep striving for excellence, we can achieve our goals and reach our full potential..

Throughout his journey, Alex remained passionate about his work and never lost sight of his goal to make a positive impact on the world. He used his success as a platform to advocate for social justice and equality, and was always willing to speak out on issues he believed in.

As Alex reached the later years of his life, he looked back on his journey with pride and gratitude. He knew that he had accomplished more than he ever thought possible, but he also recognized that none of it would have been possible without the support of those around him.

In the end, Alex's story is not just one of exceptional talent and hard work, but also one of humility, perseverance, and gratitude. He showed that even the most brilliant among us are still human, and that success is not just about what we achieve, but also about the impact we have on others.

Chapter Three

The Importance of Support: Alex's Journey with his Partner

Alex and Sarah first met in medical school, where they were both pursuing their dreams of becoming doctors. Sarah was drawn to Alex's intelligence, kindness, and dedication to his studies, and the two quickly became friends.

As they spent more time together, Sarah began to develop feelings for Alex, admiring his passion for medicine and his compassionate approach to patient care. Alex was also drawn to Sarah's intelligence and dedication to her studies, and he appreciated her support and encouragement as he navigated the rigorous demands of medical school.

Over time, their friendship blossomed into a romance, and they fell deeply in love. They supported each other through the challenges of medical school and beyond, sharing a deep bond that would endure throughout their lives.

Together, they embarked on a journey of love, partnership, and service to others, inspired by their shared commitment to making a positive impact in the world of medicine. Their love story was one of mutual respect, admiration, and devotion, and it set the foundation for a lifetime of love and partnership.

Alex and Sarah's marriage was filled with love, devotion, and a shared passion for medicine. They supported each other's careers and goals, and their partnership was a true testament to the power of love and teamwork.

As they built their life together, Alex and Sarah also started a family. They had three children who they raised with love, compassion, and a strong sense of values. Their children grew up to be accomplished and driven individuals, each pursuing their own passions in medicine, law, and public service.

Alex and Sarah were devoted parents, always making time for their children despite their demanding careers. They instilled in their children a deep sense of compassion and a commitment to making a positive impact in the world, inspiring them to follow in their footsteps and pursue careers in medicine and public service.

Throughout their marriage, Alex and Sarah shared many happy moments together. They enjoyed traveling the world, experiencing new cultures, and spending time with their family and friends. They were each other's best friend and confidante, sharing a deep bond that only grew stronger with time.

Even after Alex's passing, Sarah continued to honour his legacy and carry on his work through the foundation he established. She remained devoted to her family and continued to inspire others with her unwavering commitment to making a positive impact in the world.

The love story of Alex and Sarah was one of mutual respect, admiration, and deep devotion. Their marriage and family life were a testament to the power of love and the importance of working together to create a better world for all.

Sarah's Support during Medical School and Residency

Sarah was a constant source of love and support for Alex during his medical school and residency. She understood the demands of the profession and the sacrifices that were required to succeed, and she was always there to lend a helping hand and a listening ear.

Throughout medical school, Sarah was a dedicated partner to Alex, helping him manage the demands of his studies and providing emotional support when he needed it most. She understood the challenges he faced, and she was always there to offer encouragement and motivation to keep him going.

During his residency, Sarah continued to be a steadfast source of support. She often went above and beyond to help Alex manage his schedule and balance his responsibilities, ensuring that he had the time and energy he needed to succeed. She also provided emotional support, helping him navigate the stress and pressure of his work and providing a comforting presence when he needed it most.

Through it all, Sarah remained Alex's rock and his biggest cheerleader. She was proud of his accomplishments and inspired by his passion for medicine, and she did everything in her power to support his dreams and help him achieve his goals.

Their love and partnership were a true testament to the power of teamwork and the importance of having a supportive partner in life. Thanks to Sarah's unwavering support, Alex was able to achieve his dreams and make a meaningful impact in the world of medicine.

Sarah's support was a constant presence throughout Alex's career in medicine. As Alex's career progressed, Sarah remained his confidante, cheerleader, and partner in all aspects of his work.

When Alex established his foundation to support medical research and education, Sarah was there to help him every step of the way. She provided valuable input and guidance, helping him make strategic decisions and ensuring that the foundation's work aligned with their shared vision and values.

Throughout Alex's career, Sarah was also a key player in his professional network. She provided valuable connections and introductions, helping him build relationships with other experts in his field and expand his impact.

Sarah's support extended beyond Alex's work in medicine as well. She was a devoted partner and mother, always making time for her family despite the demands of her own career. She provided a stable, loving home for their children and served as a role model for them, demonstrating the importance of hard work, dedication, and compassion.

Despite the challenges and pressures of a career in medicine, Sarah and Alex remained deeply committed to each other and their shared vision for making a positive impact in the world. Together, they built a legacy of service, compassion, and excellence that continues to inspire others to this day.

Sarah's support for Alex extended far beyond his work in medicine. She was always there for him, providing emotional support, love, and encouragement throughout all aspects of their life together.

Whether they were facing challenges as a couple or navigating the ups and downs of parenting, Sarah was a constant presence of strength and support. She was always willing to lend an ear, offer advice, or simply provide a comforting presence when Alex needed it most.

In their free time, Sarah and Alex enjoyed traveling the world, experiencing new cultures, and making memories together as a family. Sarah was always up for an adventure, and she encouraged Alex to explore his passions and interests outside of work.

Sarah also played an active role in their community, volunteering her time and expertise to various causes and organizations. Together, she and Alex were committed to making a positive impact in the world, both through their work in medicine and through their philanthropic efforts.

Through it all, Sarah's love and support remained a constant in Alex's life. She was his partner, his confidante, and his best friend, always there to celebrate his successes and help him overcome any obstacles they faced together. Their love was a true testament to the power of teamwork and the importance of having a supportive partner in all aspects of life.

Chapter Four

Facing Setbacks

Like many successful professionals, Alex faced his fair share of failures and setbacks throughout his career. However, he was resilient and persistent, always using these challenges as opportunities to learn and grow.

When faced with failure, Alex took the time to reflect on his experiences and identify what went wrong. He then worked tirelessly to correct his mistakes and develop new strategies for success.

Throughout these struggles, Sarah was a constant source of support and encouragement for Alex. She reminded him of his strengths, provided a listening ear, and helped him stay motivated and focused on his goals.

At times, Alex also sought the help of colleagues and mentors in his field. He understood the importance of seeking guidance and learning from the experiences of others, and he was always open to feedback and constructive criticism.

Ultimately, it was Alex's determination and willingness to learn from failure that allowed him to succeed. He used his setbacks as opportunities to grow and improve, and he never let his failures define him or his career.

Thanks to his resilience and the support of Sarah and his colleagues, Alex was able to achieve great success in medicine and make a meaningful impact in the world. His story is a true testament to the power of perseverance and the importance of having a strong support system in times of challenge and adversity.

Dealing with a difficult medical diagnosis is never easy, and it can be especially challenging for those in the medical profession who are used to being the ones providing care and support to others. When faced with his own difficult diagnosis, Alex had to navigate a range of emotions and decisions, all while continuing to fulfill his professional duties.

Initially, Alex struggled to come to terms with his diagnosis. He felt a range of emotions, including fear, sadness, and anger. However, he quickly realized that he needed to take a proactive approach to his care and treatment, just as he would with one of his own patients.

With the help of Sarah and his medical colleagues, Alex sought out the best possible care and treatment options for his diagnosis. He consulted with multiple specialists, researched new treatments, and took an active role in his own care.

Throughout this process, Sarah provided unwavering support and encouragement. She accompanied Alex to his appointments, helped him navigate insurance and administrative issues, and provided emotional support whenever he needed it.

Despite the challenges of his diagnosis, Alex was able to continue working and making a meaningful impact in the field of medicine. He used his experience as a patient to deepen his understanding and empathy for those he treated, and he continued to be a source of inspiration and guidance for his colleagues.

In the end, Alex's strength and resilience in the face of his diagnosis were a testament to the power of a positive attitude and a strong support system. He was able to continue fulfilling his professional and personal responsibilities while also taking care of his own health and well-being, all thanks to the love and support of Sarah and his colleagues in medicine.

Overcoming adversity is a challenge that many people face at some point in their lives, and Alex was no exception. Throughout his career in medicine, he encountered a range of obstacles and setbacks that threatened to derail his success. However, he was able to overcome these challenges through his resilience, determination, and the support of his loved ones.

One of the biggest challenges that Alex faced was the pressure and stress of working in a high-stakes, demanding profession. He was constantly pushed to his limits, working long hours and making life-or-death decisions on a regular basis. Despite the immense pressure, Alex never wavered in his commitment to his patients and his profession.

At times, Alex also faced personal challenges that tested his resilience. He experienced the loss of loved ones, struggled with his own health issues, and faced difficult decisions in his personal life. However, he always remained focused on his goals and remained committed to pushing through the adversity.

Throughout these challenges, Sarah was a constant source of support for Alex. She provided a listening ear, offered encouragement, and reminded him of his own strengths and resilience. With her help, Alex was able to overcome each obstacle and continue making a meaningful impact in the world of medicine.

In the end, Alex's story is a testament to the power of perseverance and the importance of having a strong support system. By remaining resilient in the face of adversity and leaning on the support of those around him, Alex was able to achieve great success in his profession and make a positive impact in the world.

Chapter Five

Achievements and Contributions

As Alex's career continued to flourish, he began to receive recognition and accolades for his contributions to the medical field. He was invited to speak at conferences all over the world and was awarded numerous prestigious awards.

Despite the attention and admiration he received, Alex remained grounded and never lost sight of his values. He continued to prioritize his patients' needs above all else and worked tirelessly to provide them with the best care possible.

As he approached retirement age, Alex began to think about his legacy. He knew that his impact on the world would extend far beyond his lifetime, and he wanted to ensure that his contributions would continue to make a difference.

To that end, Driven by his passion for medicine and desire to improve patient care, Alex went above and beyond his duties as a surgeon. He established a foundation to support medical research and education, recognizing the critical role that innovation and education play in advancing medical knowledge and improving patient outcomes.

The foundation provided grants and scholarships to medical students and researchers, supporting the next generation of medical professionals and empowering them to make significant contributions to the field. Alex recognized that by investing in education and research, he could help to drive innovation and create new opportunities for medical breakthroughs that could transform the lives of patients.

In addition to providing financial support, Alex also served as a mentor and role model to aspiring medical professionals, sharing his expertise and insights to help them succeed in their own careers. He believed that by fostering a strong community of medical professionals and researchers, he could create a lasting legacy of excellence and impact in the field of medicine.

Through his foundation, Alex was able to make a meaningful difference in the lives of countless patients, researchers, and medical professionals. His dedication to improving patient care and advancing medical knowledge will continue to inspire and influence the next generation of medical professionals for years to come.

Thanks to Alex's efforts, the foundation became one of the leading organizations in the world for medical research and education. Its work has saved countless lives and continues to inspire future generations of doctors and researchers.

Throughout his career, Alex received numerous awards and recognitions for his exceptional contributions to the field of medicine. His dedication and expertise were recognized by both his peers and the wider medical community.

Among his many accolades, Alex was awarded the prestigious Nobel Prize in Medicine for his ground-breaking research into a new surgical technique that revolutionized the treatment of a previously untreatable condition. This achievement solidified his reputation as one of the world's leading experts in his field and cemented his place in medical history.

In addition to the Nobel Prize, Alex received numerous other awards and honours over the course of his career. He was named a fellow of several prestigious medical societies, including the American College of Surgeons and the Royal College of Surgeons, and was recognized with lifetime achievement awards from multiple organizations.

Alex's colleagues also recognized his exceptional contributions to the field of medicine. He was often invited to speak at conferences and was frequently sought out for his expertise and guidance. He was known for his innovative surgical techniques, his dedication to patient care, and his commitment to advancing the field of medicine through research and education.

Despite the many awards and honours he received, Alex remained humble and focused on his work. He viewed each award as a validation of his hard work and dedication, and as an opportunity to continue pushing the boundaries of what was possible in medicine.

In the end, Alex's many awards and recognitions were a testament to his exceptional talent and dedication to his profession. His contributions to the field of medicine will continue to inspire future generations of doctors and researchers for years to come.

Chapter Six

Life Beyond Medicine

As Alex looked back on his life, he realized that his success was not just the result of his own hard work and talent. He had been supported and inspired by many people along the way, from his parents to his teachers, mentors, and colleagues.

To show his appreciation, Alex made a point of staying in touch with those who had helped him and thanking them for their support. He also became a mentor himself, offering guidance and advice to young people who showed promise in medicine and other fields.

In addition to his work in medicine, Alex was also passionate about the arts. He continued to play music and create art throughout his life, seeing these pursuits as essential to his overall well-being.

Alex also remained committed to social justice and used his platform to advocate for the rights of marginalized communities. He worked with organizations dedicated to combating inequality and discrimination, and used his voice to call attention to the pressing issues of his time.

As he entered his twilight years, Alex continued to live a full and meaningful life. He spent time with his loved ones, traveled the world, and continued to pursue his interests and passions.

And when the time finally came for him to say goodbye, Alex did so with a sense of peace and fulfillment. He knew that he had lived a life of purpose and meaning, and that his legacy would continue to inspire and motivate others for generations to come.

As news of Alex's passing spread, tributes poured in from around the world. People from all walks of life, from fellow doctors and researchers to artists, musicians, and activists, spoke of the profound impact he had had on their lives.

Many noted Alex's unwavering dedication to his patients, describing him as a compassionate and caring doctor who always put their needs first. Others praised his contributions to medical research and education, citing the countless lives he had saved and the knowledge he had imparted to future generations.

Still others spoke of Alex's commitment to social justice and equality, noting his advocacy for marginalized communities and his willingness to speak out on issues that mattered.

In the days and weeks that followed, countless events were held to honor Alex's life and legacy. Medical conferences were dedicated to his memory, art galleries displayed his work, and benefit concerts were held to support causes he had cared about.

Through it all, one thing was clear: Alex's impact on the world had been immense, and his memory would continue to inspire and motivate people for generations to come.

As Alex's story comes to a close, we are reminded of the power of one person to make a difference. Through his talent, hard work, and commitment to others, Alex changed countless lives and left a lasting mark on the world. And while we may never be able to fully measure the depth of his impact, we can honour his memory by continuing his work and striving to make a difference in our own way.

Conclusion

In conclusion, Alex's story is one of remarkable perseverance and determination. Despite facing numerous obstacles throughout his life, he was able to achieve great success both personally and professionally, thanks to his unwavering dedication and hard work.

Through his story, we see that success is not just about talent or natural ability, but also about perseverance, resilience, and the willingness to work hard and push through challenges. Alex's journey serves as a reminder that with the right mindset and attitude, anything is possible.

Moreover, Alex's story is a powerful example of the importance of having a supportive network, both personally and professionally. His wife's unwavering support and encouragement played a crucial role in his success, showing that having someone who believes in us and stands by our side can make all the difference.

Ultimately, Alex's story is a source of inspiration and encouragement for anyone facing challenges in their own lives. It shows that with determination, hard work, and a supportive community, we can overcome even the greatest obstacles and achieve our dreams.

Lessons Learned

Alex's story offers several important lessons:

1. Perseverance is key: Alex faced numerous challenges and setbacks, but he never gave up on his goals. Instead, he kept pushing forward and viewed each obstacle as an opportunity to grow and learn.
2. The importance of a supportive community: Alex's wife played a crucial role in his success, providing unwavering support and encouragement throughout his journey. This highlights the importance of having a strong support network to help us navigate life's challenges.
3. Embrace failure: Alex learned to view his failures and setbacks as opportunities for growth, rather than sources of discouragement. This mindset helped him to keep pushing forward and ultimately achieve his goals.
4. Pursue your passions: Despite the demands of his career, Alex found time to pursue his passions outside of medicine, including writing and music. This serves as a reminder that it's important to make time for the things that bring us joy and fulfillment.
5. Success is not just about talent: While Alex was certainly gifted, his success was also due to his hard work, dedication, and perseverance. This highlights the fact that success is not just about natural talent, but also about the effort we put in and the mindset we bring to our work.

Final Thoughts

Alex's story is a powerful reminder of what can be achieved through perseverance, hard work, and a strong support network. Despite facing numerous obstacles and setbacks, he never lost sight of his goals and ultimately achieved great success in his career and personal life.

His story also serves as a source of inspiration and motivation for others. It shows that with determination and resilience, anything is possible, even in the face of adversity.

In reading Alex's story, we can gain valuable insights into how to navigate life's challenges and pursue our own goals and passions. We can learn from his experiences and apply these lessons to our own lives, knowing that with dedication and support, we too can achieve great things.

Overall, Alex's journey is a testament to the power of the human spirit and a reminder that we all have the potential to achieve greatness, no matter where we come from or what challenges we may face.

Acknowledgement

I would like to express my deepest gratitude to Alex and Sarah for generously sharing their story with me. Their openness, honesty, and willingness to discuss the challenges and triumphs of their journey have been truly inspiring.

I also want to thank the medical professionals, colleagues, and friends who provided valuable insights and perspectives throughout the writing process. Your expertise and support have been instrumental in bringing this book to fruition.

Special thanks to my editor and publisher, who provided guidance, encouragement, and expert advice every step of the way.

Lastly, I would like to acknowledge my family and loved ones for their unwavering support and encouragement throughout this project. Thank you all for your contributions to this book.